NEW YORK
IN
FIFTY
DESIGN
ICONS

**DESIGN
MUSEUM**

NEW YORK
IN
FIFTY
DESIGN
ICONS

**JULIE
IOVINE**

NEW YORK

INTRODUCTION

Monuments, classics and legends all make claims. They are the real thing, the permanent perfect, the unforgettable and inimitable. We look up to them from a distance. Icons are something different. They are time-bound and dynamic, intensely personal but also instantly recognizable as fragments of shared experience and memory – the aha moment made physical.

The 50 New York icons described here offer a kaleidoscopic glimpse of the city at a very particular moment: now. Though necessarily incomplete, it is a list that ranges across centuries, boroughs, styles and types – bagels as well as the Brooklyn Bridge, Louis Armstrong's turquoise Queens kitchen as well as Tiffany's blue box.

They are entirely disparate as individual stories unified by a not-so-incidental geography with a force field all its own. In fact, a surprisingly large number of these icons owe their emergence to individuals fired as much by inextinguishable determination as by prestige, cash or clout. Without the imperiously curious Phyllis Lambert, there would be no Seagram Building; the rugged primitivism of New York's water towers owe a debt to the Isseks Brothers; even the designer of the Greek paper coffee cup, Leslie Buck, has a moving backstory.

Choosing a mere 50 is a bit of a parlour game that mirrors the predilections of a generation and in particular this individual, a second-generation New Yorker who remembers the 1970s when Central Park was a no man's land and Tribeca so empty that locals – such as artists Donald Judd, Dan Flavin and friends – could play volleyball in the middle of Church Street on Sundays. My father's list would have included the Apollo in Harlem (today a non-profit theatre presenting concerts and running education and community outreach programmes) and McSorley's Old Ale House (a shadow of its beery self) on East 7th Street, whereas mine includes Judd's home at 101 Spring Street and the erstwhile punk bar CBGB's on the Bowery. My children's list will contain some different entries. As will yours. In the best way, it is a collective and ongoing story.

Called the 'Eighth Wonder of the World' and one of the largest structures in North America when it was built, the Brooklyn Bridge with its soaring gothic towers rising 83m (272ft) above the East River was completed in 1883.

BROOKLYN BRIDGE
As iconic as they come, born out of romantic optimism

As a romantic silhouette – a gargantuan harp of swooping steel cables and spreading stance of granite towers planted in bedrock – nothing beats the Brooklyn Bridge. Hailed as the greatest technological achievement and emblem of the United States' coming of age in the late 19th century, the Brooklyn Bridge remains a feat of American optimism at its most idyllically pragmatic.

Sprung straight from the heart of the American industrial revolution, the Brooklyn Bridge is probably the country's most influential bridge, and a ready subject for poets, painters, photographers and romantics, now as then.

Before the bridge, ferries carried people between Manhattan and the bustling village of Brooklyn, which was not incorporated into New York City until 1898, 15 years after the bridge opened. The bridge was envisioned by a Brooklyn entrepreneur and publisher of the *Brooklyn Eagle* and designed by a German immigrant, John Augustus Roebling, an engineer (and student of the philosopher Hegel) who set out to design the longest steel-cable suspension bridge ever attempted. Roebling died in a ferry accident in 1869 and his son, Washington Roebling, took over, adding construction innovations of his own, including the open-box caissons that allowed workmen to excavate pilings into bedrock deep under the East River. Digging at a rate of 31.5–46cm (12–18in) a week, several workers died and many, Roebling included, suffered from the earliest identified cases of the bends. Bedridden for the duration and monitoring the scene with a telescope, Roebling sent daily instructions via his wife, Emily Warren Roebling.

On 24 May 1883, New York governor Grover Cleveland, President Chester A Arthur and a multitude of thousands turned out for the bridge opening. The main span between towers stretched 486.3m (1,595.5ft) – the longest in the world until the upriver Williamsburg Bridge opened in 1903.

The Brooklyn Bridge remained the most celebrated crossing, hailed as an 'Eighth Wonder of the World'. The modernist poet Hart Crane sang the praises of its 'inviolate curve' and called it a poetry landmark; painter Joseph Stella portrayed it as emblem of a brave new world; expat author Henry James despised it as a mechanical monster that shrank the world, while, contrary to standard lore, Walt Whitman never sang its praises at all.

WATER TANKS

A necessity of urban expansion,
now a landmark on the NYC skyline

As urban icons go, the water tanks of New York seem one of the most primordial – in their rudimentary wooden materials, ubiquitous hut-like silhouettes, and sludge at the bottom of the barrel. They remain graphic holdovers from the moment when New York City burst through the barriers of being a low-rise trade town on its way to becoming a skyscraper city. That is, water tanks became necessary when buildings grew taller than six storeys, too high for the pipes channelling water down from the Adirondack reservoirs. With tanks on the roof, water could be pumped up and then gravity would do the rest to maintain water pressure below for everything from taps and toilets to fire hydrants. And they still do.

There are around 15,000 water tanks in the city – virtually all installed and maintained by two families that have been in business since the 1860s: Rosenwach Tank Company in Queens and Isseks Brothers of Manhattan. Canadian cedar is the material of choice because it is lightweight enough to haul up to the roof and because 7.6cm (3in) of wood insulates as well as 61cm (24in) of concrete. Fashioned in the same way as barrels and strapped with galvanized steel bands, the wood expands when wet to stop leaks without need for adhesives. The barrels can hold up to 37,850 litres (10,000 gallons) of water, and last as long as 35 years.

By the 20th century water tanks had become an enduring emblem of the city. In 1971 dancer and choreographer Trisha Brown composed her *Roof Piece* with dancers flitting against a backdrop of water tanks, and in 1998 British artist Rachel Whiteread, looking for something quintessentially of the city, cast a water tower in resin for her first New York installation on a rooftop in SoHo.

The original water towers were made by barrel-makers in the 1880s and are still made of wood banded in steel today.

CENTRAL PARK
The lungs of New York City, as conceived in the 1850s

There is no place in New York City more celebrated for its natural beauty than the 341-ha (843-acre) Central Park. Surprisingly, however, nature originally had very little to do with it.

The park was conceived to be the 'the lungs of the city', an antidote to the unhealthy confines of mid-19th-century urban life. According to their 1858 Greensward Plan, Frederick Law Olmsted and Calvert Vaux designed it to be a proper park modelled upon the grand estate landscapes of England: a civilizing, uplifting experience that would blot out the city.

But the site for this grand plan was something else, deemed neither commercially nor residentially viable. Barren and rocky, swollen with bogs and swamps, and rife with poison ivy, the place was described by chief engineer Egbert Viele as 'a pestilential spot, where rank vegetation and miasmatic odours taint every breath of air'.

Over 15 years of construction, every foot was reworked; every boulder placed and slope sculpted by some 20,000 labourers. Rocks were ground into gravel for the carriage drive; 270,000 trees and shrubs planted, and 4 million m³ (5 million yd³) of stone and earth hauled in from the Meadowlands and Long Island – enough to raise the park 1.2m (4ft) if it were spread evenly over the surface. Even the wilds of the Ramble, now haven to over 250 bird species (and at least as many bird watchers), are entirely artificial. Its stream runs with water that can be turned on and off like a spigot.

Central Park is a work of landscape art engineered to near perfection. One of the oldest, it is also one of the largest public works projects that the city has ever undertaken. More than 25 million people a year flock into the park, thrilled to immerse themselves in its 'natural' wonders.

The view of Central Park looking southward highlights the Harlem Meer, with the Lasker Pool and Rink adjacent to it and the 43-ha (106-acre) reservoir that was renamed the Jacqueline Kennedy Onassis Reservoir in 1994.

MILLIONAIRES' ROW

A competition of excess and extravagance

Fifth Avenue from 65th to 92nd streets is known as 'Millionaires' Row'. Here, with front-row seats on Central Park, were built the mansions of the great robber barons who monopolized industry, banking and all the raw resources young America had to mine in the late 19th and early 20th centuries. Italianate palazzos, neoclassical piles and French Renaissance palaces bore witness to the competitive wealth of the likes of Carnegie, Vanderbilt, Whitney and Astor, and in their homes they vied for the most of everything.

When Andrew 'King Steel' Carnegie built a neo-Georgian pile at 91st Street (now the Cooper Hewitt Smithsonian Design Museum), he put in one of the first residential elevators, a precursor to air conditioning, and railroad tracks in his basement to deliver coal. At 70th Street, Henry Clay Frick filled his neoclassical mansion with paintings by Rembrandt, Ingres, Renoir, Titian, Holbein, Hogarth and Gainsborough, to name but a few among other masterful flourishes, writing to a friend that he intended to 'make Carnegie's place look like a miner's shack'.

Most of the mansions of Millionaires' Row have now been demolished or institutionalized, but the Frick Collection – with all that art intact and in spite of alterations made in the 1970s (with another controversial expansion in the works) – still retains the character of a private residence offering a version of how extravagant wellbeing might once have been experienced.

Fifth Avenue was home to 'Cornelius Deux' Vanderbilt's 1883 Renaissance château, the largest home ever built in New York City. It was later demolished to make way for a department store.

Heckscher Bldg. 5th Av. and 57 St.
Copyright 1921 by Irving Underhill
N.Y.C.

CHELSEA HOTEL
New York City grandeur at its avant-garde finest

The gloriously decrepit Chelsea Hotel has been described as an 'Ellis Island of the avant-garde' and 'clubhouse for destructive geniuses'. For over a century from its opening in 1884, with its extreme curlicue iron balconies encrusting a severe Dutch red-brick façade (plus a garish neon marquee added in 1949), it has exerted a moth-like attraction for artists, bohemians, has-beens and wannabes too many to name.

Here they lived, loved, exchanged art for rent, drank (sometimes to death), consumed drugs, composed songs, wrote books, made movies, set fires, stabbed girlfriends and stole a door knob now in the collection of the Hirshhorn Museum in Washington, DC.

The Chelsea Hotel was conceived in fact as an experiment in living, based on the utopian theories of French philosopher Charles Fourier, where residents could share costs and even barter for their rent, leading eventually to the hotel's extensive art collection, much of it adorning walls and stairwells. Quite possibly, the hotel was the city's first co-op. In 1912 survivors of the *Titanic* were billeted here. But it was only after a post-war slump into a single-rooms-only for transients that the Chelsea re-emerged as a divine dive decorated in peeling plaster, 1950s tubular steel dinettes and Victorian marble mantels.

In its glory days, it was run more like a dysfunctional family than a business by a landlord, Stanley Bard, who decided who could stay and for how much, an arrangement that made well-heeled tourists underwrite needy artists. But the party was over by 2008: the place was sold to a boutique hotel chain and, in spite of a prolonged and agonized protest, even Bob Dylan's room #211 was renovated.

The hotel on West 23rd Street was built in 1884 as an experiment in cooperative living where electricians and plumbers would live side by side with artisans. By the 1940s, though, it was legendary as an artsy dive.

THE DAKOTA
From Judy Garland to John Lennon, home to the stars

The Dakota, so named because it was so far away from any place that mattered when it was built in 1884, has always stood out. Stranded on the edge of 72nd Street across from a brand-new Central Park, the Dakota was not only the city's first luxury apartment house but also, at a stately nine storeys, one of the tallest buildings in the city. A famous photograph from the 1890s shows skaters on a pond with the Dakota behind standing in splendid isolation.

It was developed by Edward Severin Clark, president of the Singer Sewing Machine Company, and designed by Henry J Hardenbergh, architect of the Plaza Hotel, in German château style. Façade ornaments play up the pioneering theme with carved arrowheads, ears of corn and the figure of a Dakota Indian over the entrance. Dragons are coiled around the cast-iron exterior railings for good measure. Loaded with luxurious innovations including its own electric generator, a wine cellar and 23-cm (9-in) layers of sand and concrete between floors for soundproofing, the Dakota was sold out before it was completed, although it attracted merchants and business folk rather than the high society that Clark had hoped for.

Ultimately, the Dakota became best known for the many artists and performers in residence, including Lauren Bacall, Leonard Bernstein, Rudolf Nureyev, Judy Garland and, most famously, John Lennon, who was shot while leaving the building on 8 December 1980. Strawberry Fields, the memorial to Lennon organized by his widow, Yoko Ono (not without controversy when members of the City Council attempted to have the spot dedicated instead to another song man, Bing Crosby), is right across the street from the Dakota in Central Park where thousands converge annually to enjoy the strawberry bushes and a mosaic, *Imagine*, donated by the city of Naples.

Completed the same year as the Chelsea Hotel in 1884, the Dakota on the Upper West Side was the city's first luxury apartment building, boasting its own wine cellar and electric generator.

FLATIRON BUILDING

A great wedge of a building, both dynamic and romantic

Never the tallest New York building but from the start one of the most inspiring to artists, the Flatiron Building is that wedge of steel, limestone and decorative terracotta forging skyward from the odd-shaped lot created where Broadway and Fifth Avenue converge and cross below Madison Square.

Almost as soon as the Flatiron was built in 1902, Alfred Stieglitz photographed it in snowy twilight, balancing a crooked tree branch against its blackened geometry. Childe Hassam painted it in numerous portraits celebrating city life. H G Wells admired the way it went 'ploughing up through the traffic' and Joseph Stella put it at the centre of his 1922 skyscraper-romancing five-panel *Voice of the City of New York Interpreted*. Then, as now, the Flatiron possessed more stature than its modest 22 storeys would suggest, embodying in its unconventional shape and Renaissance detailing the dynamic thrust and romanticism of the city as it started to flex its powers.

The Flatiron, originally named the Fuller Building, was designed by the prominent Chicago firm D H Burnham & Company (Burnham was the architectural mastermind of the 1893 World's Columbian Exposition) as the headquarters for the Fuller Construction Company. It was not always so popular with critics, who complained that there were too many windows, leaving no walls for bookcases and desks. And its early nickname, 'Burnham's Folly', hints at the temporary reluctance of New Yorkers to accept the inexorable transformation of Madison Square from a posh residential neighbourhood into a hub of commerce. Soon enough, however, the whole area became known simply as the Flatiron District.

Officially, it is the Fuller Building at 175 Fifth Avenue, designed by the Chicago architect Daniel H Burnham and completed in 1902. It became so famous that the whole neighbourhood was named after it – the Flatiron District.

YANKEE LOGO

The real symbol of New York – the Yankees'
logo is a prized sporting trademark

It is arguably the most famous logo in sports history, but unquestionably the interlocked N and Y of the Yankees' insignia, worn on cap or T-shirt, is the sign of a true New Yorker, either in the flesh or spirit. The 1909 logo not only predates the white-with-pinstripes home uniform from 1936, the oldest in Major League Baseball, but it even precedes the team name. The Yankees were known as the Highlanders after the Hilltop Park ballpark at West 168th Street where they played until 1913.

The logo's origins are a classic instance of cross-pollination in a city where money, power and style have always mixed. It was a former Irish police chief turned team owner who appropriated the distinctive lettering from an 1877 commemorative medal (honouring a policemen killed in the line of duty) that had been designed by Tiffany & Co., the luxury merchandiser.

In a sport as obsessed with traditions as it is with players' statistics, the Yankee insignia is prized above all else. (*Sports Illustrated* magazine keeps a running record of celebrities in Yankee regalia.) Or, as *New York Times* reporter Richard Morgan put it: 'The [Yankees] logo is just flat-out quintessential, distilled, pure New York.'

The team uniform is blue, white and grey but it is the interlocking logo that says it is the Yankees ever since first appearing in 1912. Here, Yankee outfielder Irv Noren sports the pinstripe home uniform in 1955.

JONES BEACH

Not the urban metropolis Robert Moses had hoped for, but his work lives on

There is no understanding New York City today without factoring in Robert Moses, the 1920s 'good government' functionary turned 1960s indomitable urban overlord, so brilliantly detailed in Robert Caro's classic 1974 tome, *The Power Broker*.

Every expressway except the East Side Drive, seven major bridges, over a thousand public housing towers, the United Nations, the Lincoln Center for the Performing Arts, 658 playgrounds and 673 baseball diamonds are just some of the projects he made happen, along with indiscriminate slum clearance, displacement of over half a million people from their homes and expenditure of over 68 billion in 1968 dollars on projects of his own devising, and almost entirely without accountability to city, state or federal government.

Moses's ultimate dreams of an infinitely expandable car-centric metropolis slashed by elevated super highways and plugged full of mega-structures were never fully realized, brought down by a middle-aged Greenwich Village lady, Jane Jacobs, who countered his Goliath-like visions with an even more powerful antidote, neighbourhood-scale community. Moses's reputation has never fully recovered.

And yet some of Moses's early accomplishments improved city life for all in still-tangible ways, especially the parkways and beaches he created in Long Island in the 1920s. There, his sensitivity to good design – stone overpasses each one different from the others, bevel-edged wooden guardrails, luxuriously proportioned parks – made good on his belief that 'nothing is too good for the people of the Empire State'. His culminating effort was the 16km (10 mile) stretch of Jones Beach on the Atlantic, created entirely out of sand dredged from Jamaica Bay with parking for over 14,000 cars, a water tank modelled on a Venetian bell tower and an 8,200-seat amphitheatre (added in 1952) with an orchestra island set off by a moat. This middle-class leisure landscape – constructed in the teeth of violent opposition from Long Island's Gatsby-esque estate owners – was entirely free to the public and of a standard, scale and quality rarely, if ever, since matched anywhere else in the world.

For more than six decades, power broker Robert Moses dominated urban planning and architecture in New York. Today he is accused of favouring cars over people, but in 1930 he cemented his fame with the stupendously popular Jones Beach State Park in Nassau County.

CHRYSLER BUILDING

A graceful beacon in New York's race for the skies

Although it held the title of 'Tallest Building in the World' for only 11 months in 1930, the Chrysler Building remains the essence and expression of confidence in technology and glamour through progress that was the skyscraper age of the early 20th century.

In New York the race to the top is a story that never disappoints. In 1929 the neo-gothic Woolworth Building (242m/794ft) had held the title for almost 17 years. Then Walter P Chrysler, the car-making titan, entered the fray determined to top it. His architect, William Van Alen, conceived a 77-storey tower that would advertise itself as the shimmering herald to the new age of the almighty automobile, clad in a novel aluminium and chrome-nickel steel, known as Enduro, that would never rust. The 319-m (1,046-ft) tower was adorned in designs taken directly from car ornaments: the eagle gargoyles (photographed so vertiginously on the 61st floor by Margaret Bourke-White) are copies of the 1929 Chrysler Plymouth hood ornament. (Van Alen based the stacked curves at the top, it has been said, on the wavy neck of a bottle of Bacardi rum that the architect saw while on a trip to Cuba.)

But as the Chrysler rose at 405 Lexington Avenue, Van Alen's own former partner, H Craig Severance, worked on a taller tower at 40 Wall Street. Van Alen retaliated, secretly embedding a 56-m (185-ft) spire within the fire shaft at the top of the Chrysler Building. A few weeks after 40 Wall Street completed construction and claimed the title of tallest building, construction workers at the Chrysler hoisted up the 6.3t (7 s.t.) so-called vertex in 90 minutes, surpassing 40 Wall by 36m (119ft). Already, however, the Empire State Building was speeding to the top using a radically new construction process – ultimately trouncing the Chrysler Building by over 62m (204ft) – and remaining the champion titleholder for 41 years. Still, the sun never sets in New York without setting the gleaming tower ablaze for a few moments like a victory torch.

At 319m (1,046ft), the Chrysler Building was the world's tallest structure for nearly one year ending in 1931. But its spire, hoisted above a frieze of hubcaps and gargoyles based on hood ornaments, has never been topped.

TISHMAN AUDITORIUM
Joseph Urban's attempt to bring the modern to the city

The Tishman Auditorium at 66 West 12th Street is one of New York's great under-celebrated modern interiors. The egg-shaped lecture hall of the New School for Social Research, with its rainbow-shaped proscenium and contracting-ring moulded walls in nine shades of grey, adds a dash of theatrical flourish to a modern sensibility newly arrived in 1930.

The auditorium was designed by the Viennese architect Joseph Urban, one of the most significant stage designers of the early 20th century, best known for his opera stagecraft and show-stopping sets for the Ziegfeld Follies. The newspaper baron William Randolph Hearst was another client and in 1929 he commissioned Urban to build the International Magazine Building on Eighth Avenue at 57th Street. (Called a 'Wagnerian funerary monument' by one critic, the six-storey structure now serves as a street-level shell and podium for Norman Foster's Hearst Tower.)

The Tishman Auditorium is the most prominent and still-intact public space within a deco-ish International Style building completed at a time when modernism was more enthusiastically embraced by academics than the man or woman on the street. Objecting to Urban's generous use of sculptural form and colour to lift the mood in classrooms and stairways, the critic Edmund Wilson sniffed that he kept expecting to see 'pretty girls in blue, yellow and cinnamon dresses to match the gaiety of the ceilings and walls'. But how appropriate for New York that it was a design impresario who helped usher in the new look of the modern.

Designed by Viennese émigré architect Joseph Urban, the Tishman Auditorium (1930) at the New School for Social Research injected an element of theatrical flair into modernism that still delivers its punch.

EMPIRE STATE BUILDING
The biggest skyscraper in the world – if not the tallest

A gorilla on any other building would never look as good. The Empire State Building has the greatest stature of any skyscraper in the world, even if it hasn't been the tallest since the 1970s. But height is not its only distinction. Designed by Shreve, Lamb & Harmon in sleekest moderne style, it started construction just weeks after the Wall Street Crash of 1929 but went on to become an unrivalled feat of engineering efficiency and speed. The 381-m (1,250-ft) building with 102 storeys was completed in just over a year, at one point adding 14 floors in ten days. In his 1932 *Men at Work,* photographer Lewis Hine recorded with awe the gasp-making balancing act of its 3,500 construction workers 'who fuse the iron of their nerves with the steel of girders'.

The equivalent of 16 storeys at the top belong to an art deco 'mooring mast' that is probably the building's most famous feature. On 16 September 1931, a private dirigible briefly moored there for 30 minutes and then, two weeks later, a Goodyear blimp managed to dock long enough to deliver the mail. But, of course, the most notorious use of the building was fictional. In the 1933 classic movie, King Kong climbed the Empire State Building and made its pinnacle his last redoubt, in this way honouring it permanently as a force of nature in its own right.

The Empire State may long ago have been knocked off its pedestal as the world's tallest building, but in the world's imagination it remains *the* iconic skyscraper.

RADIO CITY MUSIC HALL
The jewel of Rockefeller's grand vision

Mega-structures have a dystopian ring, redolent of beetling charcoal-dark towers glowering in the up-lights and people dwarfed to ant-like dots. It is easy to forget that Rockefeller Center is one of them. With its layering of plazas and pavilions, endless underground passages and some 20 buildings arrayed like a guard of honour around the soaring RCA (now NBC Universal) Building, the Rockefeller Center remains surprisingly user-friendly, thanks to an extraordinary attention to detail. Nowhere is this more appealingly in evidence than at Radio City Music Hall, the first building to be completed and the jewel of the original complex constructed in 1931–2.

Financed by John D Rockefeller and masterminded by S L 'Roxy' Rothafel, Radio City Music Hall with its 6,000 seats was to be a people's palace for 'super-vaudeville' acts, live broadcasts and movies. Under the supervision of Edward Durell Stone, an architect of the Museum of Modern Art, Donald Deskey – who packaged Crest toothpaste among other everyday products – marshalled a battalion of artisans and painters to jazz up the interiors in art deco style. Walls were made of Bakelite and patent leather; fixtures and railings of nickel and sleek stainless steel; armchairs in pony hide. The men's lounge was wallpapered in a 'nicotine'-coloured foil provided by the R J Reynolds Tobacco Company and decorated with a mural, *Men Without Women* by Stuart Davis, the American Ashcan modernist. It was the acme of bootlegger glam and antidote to the disaster at the RCA Building that was the communist artist Diego Rivera's mural of workers, war machinery and Lenin, among other hot topics, that Rockefeller had destroyed before it was completed.

Radio City Music Hall has maintained its sheen, especially after a $30-million renovation in 1999, kept afloat, no doubt, by the precision kicks of the Rockettes, an enduring tradition in cheesecake since opening night on 27 December 1932.

At the heart of Rockefeller Center, Radio City Music Hall still glints in art deco splendour, with the three-storey-high *Fountain of Youth* mural by Ezra Winter cascading down the lobby's grand staircase.

GUGGENHEIM MUSEUM

Controversial at birth, now an established
wonder of American architecture

The Solomon R Guggenheim Museum is the only building in New York by the man most often called the country's greatest architect, Frank Lloyd Wright. It took him 16 years, six full sets of plans and 749 drawings to get it built. And the Guggenheim remains one of the most controversial and singular museums in the world, both loved and loathed by visitors, artists and curators.

The project got under way in the early 1940s when Solomon Guggenheim, a philanthropist and an heir to the family's mining fortune, decided to build a home for his non-objective painting collection amassed with the help of his colourful German confidante and artistic guide, Baroness Hilla von Rebay. More than any mere icon, Rebay wrote to Wright that she was commissioning him to design the 'expression of the cosmic breath itself' and 'a temple of spirit, a monument'. He promised her all that and more, adding that his museum would be so ambitious that people 'may be at first shocked or offended'.

They were. Both city officials and artists took offence at the earliest plans revealing a coiled spring of a moulded concrete structure with a quarter-mile ramp at a steep rake lined with tilted walls for showing art as if on an easel. At the first press conference in 1945 Wright bragged: 'When the first atom bomb lands on New York [the museum] will not be destroyed; it may be blown a few miles up into the air, but when it comes down it will bounce.'

The *New York Times* published an editorial 'aghast' at the museum's shape, describing it as an 'oversized and indigestible hot cross bun'. Artists wrote an open letter to the museum's trustees calling it 'unsuitable for a sympathetic display of painting and sculpture'. Among those who signed were Willem de Kooning, Franz Kline and Robert Motherwell.

Frank Lloyd Wright died six months before the museum's official opening on 21 October 1959. Five months later a survey of 500 leading architects ranked it as the 18th wonder of American architecture.

On its opening in 1959, newspapers called the Guggenheim Museum 'the most controversial building ever to rise in New York'. Its architect, Frank Lloyd Wright, claimed it was not a museum but an 'Archeseum'.

UNITED NATIONS LOBBY
The art of international bureaucracy

Although a landmark of the highest visibility in New York, the United Nations is not actually of the city but rather an independent territory jointly owned by over 200 member states. The complex is a near-perfect manifestation of confident bureaucracy, cooperative compromise, glamorous style and other mid-century-modern virtues. To the scale-free rectilinear rigidity of the Secretariat, the bow-sided, swoop-roofed General Assembly Building introduced some much-needed sex appeal. No place says it better than the General Assembly lobby, completed in 1952, where boomerang-shaped, bone-white balconies do not so much float as hover around a monumental clearing at least three storeys tall, tethered only by a blue steel stair hiked up by a cast-iron arc opposite towering channels of translucent glass meant to spread cathedral-soft light throughout.

The space so perfectly captured the era's sense of bravura performance that Alfred Hitchcock chose it for a pivotal scene in his classic suspense film *North by Northwest* (1959). When he could not secure permits to film on location, Hitchcock used hidden cameras to get the outside of the building as Cary Grant rushes in and matte-painting backdrops based on still photographs for the lobby interiors. The long-distance shots minimize the deception and succeed brilliantly at broadcasting the monumental verve and energy of the space. Zaha Hadid has described the lobby balconies as an inspiration for her own penchant for curves. Following a $2.2-billion renovation of the entire complex, the General Assembly lobby reopened to the public in September 2014 in time for the 69th annual session.

Thirteen internationally renowned architects worked on the United Nations, among them Le Corbusier, Oscar Niemeyer and Wallace K Harrison, but the most famous name associated with it is that of film director Alfred Hitchcock, for setting a scene in his spy thriller, *North by Northwest*, in the General Assembly lobby.

LEVER HOUSE
The dawn of the modern corporate façade

The Lever House is a linchpin in the history of tall buildings. Curiously modest at 21 storeys – its sea-green glass slab occupying only a fraction of the site and turned sideways to present just 16m (53ft) on Park Avenue – Lever House, completed in 1952, launched the glass-curtain-wall office building as the golden standard of the corporate world.

It was designed by Gordon Bunshaft – the lead designer at Skidmore, Owings & Merrill, a post-war architectural partnership specializing in international modernism (and derided by some as the 'three blind Mies') – for the Lever Brothers Company, a soap and household products manufacturer.

While the United Nations Secretariat, completed a year before, is also a slab building, it has two solid masonry façades, while Lever House is entirely crystalline with glass banded in stainless steel on all sides. The slab floats atop a one-storey podium itself hollowed out around an open courtyard and supported on slender columns. Rather than encountering a solid wall along Park Avenue, pedestrians were given access to stroll across the courtyard and into exhibition spaces – showing everything from cleaning products to art works – in the lobby.

While some critics decried its assault on the continuous masonry wall of Park Avenue, the Lever House was instantly celebrated as a new landmark, with *Business Week* magazine calling it 'spacious, efficient and washable' in 1954. Indeed, one of its longest-lasting distinctions was the invention of a gondola-rigged window-washing mechanism suspended from the roof on a track that is still the basic model used today – the ideal legacy for a soap company.

The Lever House, designed by Skidmore, Owings & Merrill as the headquarters for a soap company, represented the epitome of corporate cool for mid-century Manhattan. Facing sideways to the avenue was only part of it.

SEAGRAM BUILDING
A block of Bauhaus in the heart of the city

The Seagram Building (1958) embodies the gathering momentum of post-war American power and the mobilization of ambition, confidence, money and ability by a 27-year-old heiress.

Dedicated to the cause of modern architecture, Phyllis Lambert, née Bronfman, reacted in horror when her father, Samuel Bronfman, head of the Canadian distillery dynasty, revealed lacklustre plans for 375 Park Avenue (Her exact words were, 'No, no, no, no, no…'). An art student in Paris at the time, Lambert quickly took over, insisting that the new HQ must represent no less than 'the best of the society in which we live'. Ignoring Frank Lloyd Wright's pitch for a 100-storey monolith, she chose cigar-chomping Ludwig Mies van der Rohe, the Bauhaus architect and virtuoso designer of austere strengths and luxurious finishes whose motto 'Architecture is the real battleground of the spirit' both cowed and inspired generations of architects.

At 157m (515ft) and 38 storeys, Seagram is neither the tallest (still the Empire State Building until 1972) nor the first International Style skyscraper in America (that would be the Philadelphia Saving Fund Society of 1932). But Seagram has retained its aura as the most fully realized and still glamorous expression of corporate aspiration. The gleaming bronze slab is one of the first where glass is not a window pane but a skin. The Seagram tower rises from a plaza where symmetrical square pools bracketed by elongated verde-granite seating, choreographed gingko trees and tooled stone paving coordinate as smoothly as in a Zen garden.

The interiors are no less renowned, specifically the Four Seasons restaurant, canteen for the cosmopolitan business crowd, outfitted with sombre sensuality by Philip Johnson, a former curator of the Museum of Modern Art and later architecture's nosiest *éminence grise*. Both exterior and restaurant interior were granted landmark status in 1989.

Neither the tallest nor the first International Style skyscraper in New York, the Seagram Building designed by Mies van der Rohe is indisputably the most exquisitely detailed.

LINCOLN CENTER
Launched with a presidential seal of
approval to usher in a new cultural age

At the ground-breaking in May 1959, flanked by urban mastermind Robert Moses and with Leonard Bernstein conducting the New York Philharmonic and 12,000 well-wishers in attendance, President Eisenhower made no small claims for the new Lincoln Center for the Performing Arts: 'Here will develop a mighty influence for peace and understanding throughout the world' heralding 'America's cultural coming of age'.

His were not the only sights set high. Moses had identified the slummy but bohemian neighbourhood (home to the likes of Thomas Hart Benton, Edward Hopper and Eugene O'Neill) on the Upper West Side as ideal for one of his massive slate-cleaning projects. John D Rockefeller III, as president of the new centre, saw his chance to spur the United States' international reputation in the arts. To that end, he gathered together a dream team of world-renowned architects to design what was essentially a one-stop high-culture venue welcoming to the middle classes.

Wallace K Harrison was technically in charge but let the talent hash out their differences while he focused on designing the indisputable centrepiece, the Metropolitan Opera House. His partner, Max Abramovitz, designed the Philharmonic Hall. While Alvar Aalto and Marcel Breuer departed early, Eero Saarinen and Gordon Bunshaft remained on board. Philip Johnson joined at the request of choreographer George Balanchine, to design the New York State Theater where Balanchine performed. The only thing they all agreed on was the building material, white travertine, because of its associations with ancient Rome.

Ultimately, the three main performance spaces were arranged around an open plaza with a fountain – inspired by Michelangelo's Piazza del Campidoglio – on a plinth that seemed to shear into a cliff at the back of the complex. Even as it was excoriated for being isolated from street life and confounding to negotiate, Lincoln Center achieved its goal, if not as a lodestar of world peace, then definitely as the white-hot nucleus of the city's performing arts scene. In 2013 a redesign completed by Diller Scofidio + Renfro solved many persisting circulation and access problems.

Conceived in the mid-1950s as an arts complex for the middle classes, Lincoln Center was initiated by John D Rockefeller, whose dreams of a new opera house at Rockefeller Center had been thwarted in the 1930s.

STONEWALL INN
The gay bar that sparked a liberation movement

Long before the letters LGBT signalled anything, there was Stonewall Inn at 51–53 Christopher Street. It was a dumpy nondescript joint in Greenwich Village but events here launched the gay liberation movement.

Originally a stables then a speakeasy in the 1930s, Stonewall Inn was turned into a gay bar by the Mafia in 1966. It was the largest gay bar in the city and the only one that allowed dancing. Inside, there was a long black plywood bar sturdy enough to support cross-dressing go-go dancers, a jukebox and a light bulb dangling from the ceiling that flashed to alert patrons to the frequent police raids. But on the night of 28 June 1969 when some half-dozen police officers turned up, the patrons refused to budge and a riot broke out that lasted three days. However spontaneous and disorganized, it was the first time that gay, lesbian, bisexual and transgender people and Villagers all united in common cause, and the world took notice. Within two years, there were gay rights groups in every major city in the United States and in many other countries worldwide.

Stonewall Inn itself lost its lease just three months later. A variety of local businesses occupied the space; renovations and alterations were made but the spot has remained a touchstone site for gay people who set out from Christopher Street every June for one of the wildest, most inspired annual parades in the city. In 2000 Stonewall Inn was made a National Historic Landmark.

The riot at Stonewall Inn on Christopher Street in June 1969 not only triggered the gay rights movement but also an annual summer parade down Fifth Avenue that ends in Greenwich Village.

MACY'S THANKSGIVING DAY PARADE BALLOONS

The pride of Thanksgiving – as seen by 50 million people

What is six storeys tall, 9m (30ft) wide and 18m (30ft) long? Any kid at heart in New York City knows the answer: Macy's Thanksgiving Day Parade balloons.

Of the over 50 balloons, 'falloons' (float balloons) and 'balloonicles' (mobile balloons), the largest, character balloons – whether Kermit the Frog, Snoopy, Dora the Explorer or Spiderman – are so huge (weighing a minimum of 54kg/120lb) that each one takes up to 70 handlers to keep them tethered and afloat during the parade's three-hour march to Macy's home in Herald Square.

The legendary parade, made even more famous by the 1947 Christmas classic, *Miracle on 34th Street*, first took place on 27 November 1924. It was organized by Macy's employees and, for the first few years, it started in Harlem at 145th Street rather than at the Natural History Museum on Central Park West. Originally, the parade included floats and camels, donkeys, elephants and goats from the Central Park Zoo with Santa Claus bringing up the rear on the last float, an ongoing tradition. But in 1927 the live animals were replaced by rubber balloons. The first character was Felix the Cat, made by a marionette maker. In 1934 Mickey Mouse made his debut, while Donald Duck arrived only in 1962. Today the chosen characters are an annual litmus test of pop-culture icons.

Most of the balloons are fabricated in a former Tootsie Roll factory, called Macy's Parade Studio, in Hoboken. Consultants in engineering and aerodynamics calculate the character's flying pattern – vertical, horizontal or in between. Painted clay models are made to scale before the fabric is cut. The balloons were made of rubber up until World War II but are now made of polyurethane, with multiple chambers for holding 340–396m³ (12,000–14,000ft³) of helium.

The Macy's Thanksgiving Day Parade is attended by some 3.5 million people and watched by over 50 million more on television. But for many New Yorkers the most memorable event takes place the night before the parade, when people are allowed to gather at 77th Street and Columbus Avenue to watch the gargantuan figures come to life as they are inflated through the night.

The most famous balloons at the Macy's Thanksgiving Day Parade have included Mickey Mouse, introduced in 1934, Popeye in 1957, Kermit the Frog in 1977 (below) and seven versions of Snoopy since 1968.

LOUIS ARMSTRONG'S BLUE KITCHEN

A pilgrimage site for jazz enthusiasts, and a slice of American history

With his signature raspy voice and transcendent trumpet riffs, Louis Armstrong made jazz immediate, irresistible and personal for generations of music lovers. His nicknames, 'Satchmo' and 'Pops', capture the downhome magic of this legendary superstar who died in 1971 but lives forever. So does his turquoise kitchen.

When Armstrong was already famous and the world was his stage, he and his wife Lucille Wilson wanted to keep it simple and put down roots in working-class Corona, Queens, in 1943. The red-brick row house on 107th Street was nondescript until the couple went for an all-out makeover in the 1960s. Since he was a New Orleans boy through and through, the kitchen was the heart and soul of the place, and it had to make a splash.

All the cabinetry was lacquered cool blue, with 'bullseye' white lacquer and stainless-steel knobs; the stove was a custom double oven with an inscribed dedication plaque from the manufacturer. A red blender was built into the counter, as were the aluminium foil and wax-paper dispensers. A window shelf for plants was made of thick clear Lucite and the walls were papered with a silkscreen Japanese-style abstract print of cherry blossom trees inspired by the couple's Japanese garden. And it is all still there. The Louis Armstrong House Museum is a hidden gem in Queens that jazz lovers have flocked to since it opened in 1993 for tours as well as the occasional performance. An expanded visitor centre, rehearsal space for musicians and even a jazz club are coming.

The trumpet-playing jazz legend loved his rice and beans and his wife, Lucille Wilson, made the dish New Orleans-style in an ice-blue cool kitchen in their Queens home, now a museum.

TWA TERMINAL
A monument to the romantic heyday of air travel

Was there really a time when air travel was experienced as a cosmopolitan jaunt where chicly dressed stewardesses served ice-tinkling cocktails in comfortably padded cabins with the latest in mid-century décor? Proof that it once was truly so can still be found in the swooped-up wings of the TWA Terminal at John F Kennedy International Airport. Designed by Eero Saarinen & Associates in 1956 and built in 1962, the TWA Terminal is a remarkably coherent work of architectural art – not to mention flair – where handrails, departure boards, sidewalk overhangs and even the air vents all adhere to a single aesthetic vision of modernism as a dynamic freeform sculpture.

One of the leading lights of mid-century modernism, Saarinen refused to adhere to straight lines as dictated by modernist dogma. He said of the TWA Terminal that 'the shapes were deliberately chosen in order to emphasize an upward-soaring quality of line. We wanted an uplift.' And it delivered.

However, times changed: the ticketing desks operated too much like a luxury hotel concierge; the sidewalk sheltered by an ingeniously engineered concrete curve was too narrow to cope with new security challenges; the entire space was functionally unresponsive to the new demands of cattle-call-style travel. (Trans World Airlines itself did not survive the transition.) When the building was designated a historic landmark in 1994, it was transformed, as far as the airport authorities were concerned, from soaring eagle to albatross. Closed to air travel in 2001, it reopened briefly as a gallery and event space. After that, it was incorporated into a much larger JetBlue terminal as a detour for nostalgic travellers with spare time. By 2013 it had closed again, awaiting a new plan, still pending, to try the space out as a swanky hotel.

Mid-century architect Eero Saarinen refused to be tied down by prevailing trends in the rectilinear lines of International Style modernism, moulding concrete into highly sculptural forms loaded with metaphorical brio.

BAGEL
Feeding New Yorkers for well over a hundred years

New York City mothers have been known to warn their children to never to eat a bagel from outside the city limits – such is the conviction that only the city's boiled-and-baked bagels are the real thing.

From the first major waves of Eastern European immigrants in 1880s to the ascendance of bagel-making machinery in 1960s, the long heyday of the NYC bagel is now past and only diehards can identify for certain the true shiny and pliant crust; the connection joint proving the ring was hand-rolled; and the tangy dense taste of slow-fermented dough within.

But the memory is legend – cemented at such local pilgrimage stops as H&H Bagel on the Upper West Side and broadcast far and wide in Woody Allen films as well as episodes of *Seinfeld*, *Friends* and *Sex and the City*. Both the H&H shop on Broadway, where the smell of bagels once perfumed the sidewalks 24 hours a day, and its midtown factory were shuttered by 2012 due to tax fraud and other financial misdoings.

There are other bagels in the world: in Montreal, the bagels are sweeter with a touch of malt and honey; the ones found in London's Golders Green are harder with air bubbles. And then there are the baked puffballs that should fool no one, however ubiquitous. In recent years, young bakers have tried again to plumb the secret of the inimitable flavour of the true NYC bagel. Maybe it is in the water.

Whether with lox or a cream-cheese schmear, the New York City bagel is legendary. The ovens at H&H Bagels, famous bakers on the Upper West Side, may now be cold, but artisanal ovens are heating up in Brooklyn.

2 COLUMBUS CIRCLE

A success story the second time around

Only 12 storeys tall, 2 Columbus Circle, current home of the Museum of Arts and Design (MAD), has attracted more controversy than its diminutive size would seem to warrant.

In truth, it represents perhaps more of a flashpoint than an icon in the combative arena that is New York City. Stout and windowless, 2 Columbus Circle was born as the Gallery of Modern Art in 1964. It was the pet project of Huntington Hartford, an heir to a supermarket chain and art-collecting playboy who prided himself on going against the tide. His collection consisted of out-of-fashion figurative paintings by Salvador Dalí, Edward Burne-Jones and Édouard Vuillard. His architect was Edward Durell Stone, a notable name (Radio City Music Hall, Museum of Modern Art, US Embassy in Delhi) in semi-disgrace for straying from pure modernism into decorative flourishes.

When the gallery opened in 1963, *New York Times* architecture critic Ada Louise Huxtable dismissed the white marble building with its filigreed portholes as 'a die-cut Venetian palazzo on lollipops'. The gallery failed; subsequent occupants, including a university department, government office and nightclub, did not last long either. The unloved structure stood abandoned for some seven years. Then, in 2005, MAD bought the lease and proposed stripping it down to its most essential concrete and rebuilding it as an iridescent ceramic box, designed by an emerging star architect, Brad Cloepfil. Suddenly, the preservation community, architecture buffs and NIMBY neighbours rallied to its defence. Alas, the building had been passed over definitively for landmark status in 1996 before mid-century modern had achieved its current historic cachet. Then as now, however, there are few more stunning views of the city than those from the penthouse restaurant.

In its first incarnation, the curved and diminutive 2 Columbus Circle was dismissed for its cut-rate Venetian-palazzo styling but now re-clad in iridescent white bricks it seems to have achieved more respect.

101 SPRING STREET (DONALD JUDD'S HOUSE)

The city's final single-use cast-iron building

Before it was SoHo, the blocks south of Houston Street were known as the Cast Iron District, and the last cast-iron building dedicated to a single use was at 101 Spring Street, the home of minimalist artist Donald Judd.

Judd bought the five-storey 1871 building, formerly full of machine shops, in 1968 because he liked its unusual blend of historic 'fancy' façade and modern multitude of glass windows, so many that he called it 'the furthest forerunner of the curtain-wall'. Judd approached the renovation by purposely leaving spaces largely undone. Yet what he did do was telling.

Each floor was dedicated to a single purpose – eating, sleeping, working – and filled with artworks by Judd's friends, including Claes Oldenburg, Frank Stella and Dan Flavin. The furnishings were intentionally bare-boned classics by Alvar Aalto, Gerrit Rietveld and Judd himself. His own thinking about art was everywhere apparent, for instance in the way that the oak floorboards on one of the floors are mirrored in the oak ceiling to look like parallel planes, or the precisely graduated spacing between kitchen shelves from 5cm to 31.5cm (2–12in) to accommodate flatware to bowls.

Judd spent 25 years on and off at 101 Spring Street but ultimately chose the wide open space of Marfa, Texas, to expand his sculptural expression to the size of an entire town. In 2013, following a $23-million renovation, 101 Spring Street reopened to allow the public in (by appointment only) to see the place still looking much as it did when Judd lived and worked there.

Minimalist artist Donald Judd turned parts of his own home into conceptual artworks, including one storey's parallel planes in oak for floor and ceiling. Below, the cast-iron loft building at 101 Spring Street in SoHo.

WHITNEY MUSEUM

A brooding study in brutalism

With a shape suggesting an upside down ziggurat, the Whitney Museum of American Art was described as 'Mesopotamian Modern' when it opened in 1966, 'a miniature Alcatraz on Madison' (by a critic who actually admired it) and the 'Madison Avenue Monster'. People did not know what to make of the glowering grey façade with just one window protruding at a cocky angle, an entrance that sat across a 10.6-m (35-ft) bridge overlooking a moat filled with sculpture, and an 26-m (85-ft) sheer wall of rough-and-ready, board-formed concrete cutting it off from the brownstones next door. The architect, Bauhaus-trained, Harvard-based Marcel Breuer, wanted his building isolated to 'emphasize the completeness of the architectural form' as a sculpture on its own terms. But neighbours called it rudely out of context.

The severe sculptural profile of the Whitney belongs to the late modern moment in architecture called brutalism, known for brooding concrete forms and monumental geometries that are often challenging to love. But the Whitney's appropriately contextual size and the lavish attention paid by the architect to its detailing gentled its severity, and within a relatively short time the Upper East Side and all New York came to appreciate how the Whitney stands out as distinctively modern. In fact, many welcomed the Whitney for aggressively scoring one for culture over commerce, the reigning preoccupation along Madison Avenue. The architect and critic Peter Blake described it bluntly as 'Art's answer to the huckster'.

Ultimately, no fewer than four subsequent efforts to expand the museum (by such worthies as Michael Graves, Rem Koolhaas and Renzo Piano) all failed amid an uproar over tampering with Breuer's signatory masses. In 2010 the Whitney decided to move downtown altogether and allow the Metropolitan Museum of Art to take over the 54-year-old landmark, now considered a significant stripe in the historic fabric of New York.

When the Whitney Museum with its one Cyclops eye opened on Madison Avenue in 1966, it was met with public derision, but in later years the neighbourhood would let no alterations mar its singular top-heavy form, below.

58

ONE CHASE MANHATTAN PLAZA

Surreal and abstract, Plop Art provides
the perfect photo op

Across New York there are hundreds of important bronze men on pedestals and other impressive figures from the Statue of Liberty in the harbour to Balto the sled dog in Central Park. And there is Plop Art.

Plop Art was the term affixed to the often abstract outdoor public art first envisioned in the late 1960s and 1970s as a salubrious way to enliven public spaces, engage corporate donors and support New York's reputation as a centre of the art world. Jean Dubuffet's towering and cartoon-like *Group of Four Trees* (1972) at One Chase Manhattan Plaza in Lower Manhattan is one of the earliest and most successful examples of the form.

In 1969 the banker and philanthropist David Rockefeller commissioned the French artist Dubuffet to create a sculpture for the Chase Bank plaza, where a sunken water garden designed by Isamu Noguchi was already located since the 1962 completion of the austere modernist slab by Skidmore, Owings & Merrill. At the dedication, Dubuffet, who described his *Four Trees* as drawings rather than sculptures, said that he wanted to capture the city's 'impression of feverish intoxication' and 'to manifest the ardent source of the enormous intellectual machinery of which this plaza is the core'.

While another large-scale site-specific work of public art, Richard Serra's *Tilted Arc* (1981), was removed amid controversy from a downtown plaza in 1989, *Group of Four Trees* has remained one of the most popular photo opportunities in the city.

In 2014 new Chinese owners renamed the building after its address, 28 Liberty Street, considered a lucky number and a propitious reference to the statue in the harbour. Jean Dubuffet's *Four Trees,* however, did not waver.

1972 SUBWAY MAP

Massimo Vignelli's attempt to rationalize
the NYC subway

As patterns go, it was elegantly modern: strands of electrified primary colour gathered in bundles knotted with black dots that ran with smooth geometric rationale at 45-degree angles or elongated vectors across a landscape of beige fields and a grey square. But as a legible guide to New York's tortuously complex underground rail system, the 1972 subway map was a complete failure. Straphangers complained about its 'geographical inaccuracies' and called it 'aesthetically confusing', and it was discontinued within a few years. But, among graphic designers and design buffs, it is legend.

The 1972 subway map was designed by the Italian-born graphic designer Massimo Vignelli with assistance from his wife, Lella Vignelli, and Dutch graphic designer Bob Noorda, a team that helped invent the concept of corporate identities in the 1960s. The Vignelli name is behind such timeless logos as the inflight chevrons of American Airlines, the sans-serif Bloomingdale's and Knoll's red. For the New York subway map, Vignelli was inspired by Harry Beck's abstract map for the London Underground. It all made perfect sense: true scale was disregarded so that congested Midtown could be enlarged for clarity and the outer boroughs telescoped. Above-ground geography was ignored; that grey square in Manhattan was rectangular Central Park.

Out of print, it was already a classic, collected by tourists as a souvenir and praised as an icon of modernity by graphic designers such as Stephen Heller who admired the way it 'bypassed the literal details and focused on the relationships inherent in the information – less is more'. The rest of Vignelli's concept – using a clean and modern Helvetica typeface printed in white on black signs and rationally located where travellers are most likely to need the information – remains in use today.

In 2004 the Museum of Modern Art added the original diagram of the 1972 subway map along with the design team's entire graphic standards manual to its design collection. And, in 2012, the Vignellis were invited back by the Metropolitan Transit Authority to adapt their map for use as the MTA phone app.

On an average weekday, 5.5 million people ride the New York City subway system. A masterpiece of logic, Vignelli's 1972 map was discontinued after seven years due to customers' complaints that it was too confusing.

System Map

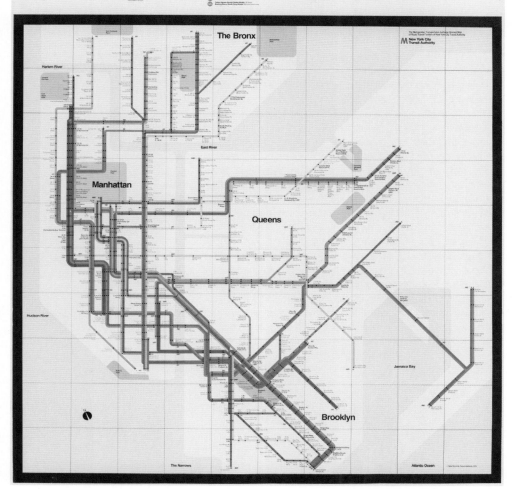

How To Use This Map

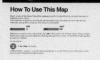

Key

IRT

IND

BMT

The Bronx

Harlem River

Manhattan

East River

Queens

Hudson River

Jamaica Bay

Brooklyn

The Narrows

Atlantic Ocean

The Metropolitan Transportation Authority Honored Map
of Transit Facilities of New York City Transit Authority

New York City
Transit Authority

CBGB

The beating heart of the New York punk scene

Most commonly seen now on the streets of New York, and the world, as an aggressive funhouse graphic on T-shirts, CBGB back in the day was a Bowery bar, a mecca, a legend, and the viciously contentious birthplace of American punk rock.

In 1973 Hilly Kristal, a sad-sack ex-hippie with an ear for music, opened a venue in a former flophouse on a seedy stretch of the Lower East Side that he hoped would become known for country, bluegrass and blues, thus the acronym name. (A subtitle, '& OMFUG', stood for 'and Other Music for Uplifting Gourmandizers'.) That never happened. The bands that did start trickling, then stampeding, stomping, carousing and tearing up the place, acoustically and literally, made the sound of a revolution in music: Patti Smith, the Ramones, Blondie, the Dead Boys, Talking Heads, the Sex Pistols, the Cramps, the Dictators, Guns N' Roses. On and on for three ear-splitting decades, CBGB spotlighted the music and provided the right ambience – raunchy, indestructible and liberating.

A legion of punk aficionados lovingly recall not only the music but also the sordid toilets, brawls, drugs and Kristal's incontinent pet dog, as well as his generosity in hiring addicts and the homeless to be short-order cooks and sound technicians. For emerging punks, it was Wonderland painted black. The scene moved on; the place on 315 Bowery closed down in 2006 followed by a few stabs at resurrection as a retail shop and a music and film festival (still running). In 2013 CBGB was elected to the National Register of Historic Places with a citation commemorating its role as 'cultural incubator'.

The Bowery dive did not set out to be a punk haven for the likes of Patti Smith, the Ramones and the Sex Pistols. Founder Hilly Kristal wanted to feature country, bluegrass and blues, but only the acronym remains as testament.

GRAND CENTRAL STATION
New York's cathedral to travel

Some 750,000 people charge through Grand Central Terminal daily but one of the most consequential assemblages of people beneath the station's zodiac-studded vaults took place on 30 January 1975.

It was then that Jacqueline Kennedy Onassis, Mayor Robert Wagner, novelist Louis Auchincloss, architect Philip Johnson and members of the Municipal Arts Society held a press conference in the Oyster Bar to protest against a recent decision by the state supreme court to allow the railroad to develop the air rights over the glorious, if faded, Beaux-Arts beauty. Demolishing and developing around the terminal had been bruited about for a decade. In 1956 the architect I M Pei proposed to replace the station with an 80-storey Chinese finger-puzzle 'Hyperboloid'. But now the threat was from a 59-storey tower that would float atop the grand concourse, with 52 elevators pummelling down through the main waiting room, to be designed by the Bauhaus-trained Marcel Breuer.

Galvanized by the public outcry – stirred to boiling by the presence of Mrs Onassis – the Landmarks Preservation Commission took its appeal all the way to the US Supreme Court, which in 1978 upheld the Landmarks Law – a major preservation victory and precedent for the entire nation. In June 2014 a plaque commemorating Mrs Onassis's role was dedicated at the main entrance to the station on Park Avenue. But perhaps the words of Philip Johnson spoken at that 1975 press conference best capture New Yorkers' attitude: 'Europe has its cathedrals and we have Grand Central Station.'

Haunted by the demolition of another Beaux-Arts stunner, Pennsylvania Station, in 1963, the New York community rallied to save Grand Central Station, in the process giving birth to the national preservation movement in 1978.

TEMPLE OF DENDUR

A slice of ancient Egypt, nestled within the
Metropolitan Museum of Art

There are New York destinations – the Statue of Liberty, the observation deck of the Empire State Building, the latest musical revival on Broadway – that seem to belong more to tourists than to city dwellers. But not the Temple of Dendur at the Metropolitan Museum of Art. This compact ancient Egyptian sanctuary, commissioned by the Roman emperor Augustus around 15 BCE, has been the favourite go-to location for charity galas and first dates since it opened to the public in 1978.

The Temple of Dendur, 8m (26ft) tall, comprised of 5.4-t (6-s.t.) blocks of sandstone rich in ancient carvings and 18th-century graffiti, was the oversized thank-you gift from the Egyptian government to the United States for help with the Aswan Dam in 1965. The competition for this Nubian trophy was so stiff that newspapers at the time called it the Dendur Derby. Washington, DC thought it should sit along the Potomac River as it had along the Nile; Boston wanted it for the Charles River; Cairo, Illinois felt it had a claim, as did Memphis, Tennessee. On 27 April 1967 it was announced that the Metropolitan Museum of Art had been chosen. Architects Kevin Roche, John Dinkeloo and Associates built an entire wing to house the temple so that it could be oriented east-west as it had been in Egypt, with a reflecting pool suggesting the Nile, and a canted rear wall reminiscent of cliffs nearby. Even the lighting is designed to mimic the diffused light and desert sky of Nubia. It is the ultimate period room.

The largest exhibit at the Metropolitan Museum of Art, the Temple of Dendur was rescued from the flooding Nile upon the construction of the Aswan Dam in 1965, and presented to the United States as a gift from the Egyptian government.

BELL 47D-1 HELICOPTER

Efficiency and beauty combine in New York's own *Winged Victory*

By adding a helicopter to its design collection in 1984, the Museum of Modern Art found a particularly forcible way to show that design goes well beyond chairs, buildings and products.

As described by the MoMA acquisition report, the Bell 47D-1 is 'an object whose delicate beauty is inseparable from its efficiency'. More than 3,000 were manufactured in Buffalo, New York, between 1945 and 1973. What set the Bell 47 apart were the seamless bug-eyed glass bubble canopy and exposed trellis tail boom that metamorphosed the purely functional into an emblem of dynamic grace. The helicopter was designed by Arthur M Young, a maths and engineering savant, who as a young boy in rural Pennsylvania built a crane from a Meccano Erector set that was capable of hoisting his brother. Later at Princeton, he studied maths, philosophy and theories of the universe before settling on a plan to design helicopters. In 1941 Young joined Bell Aircraft and developed the Bell 47, the world's first commercial helicopter.

Arthur Drexler, the long-time director of the Department of Architecture and Design at MoMA, obtained the helicopter and suspended it over a narrow staircase, believing it would draw people up to the sometimes overlooked department. In the 2004 expansion of the museum by architect Yoshio Taniguchi, the helicopter was given pride of place, hovering over the grand staircase to the second floor. Terence Riley, then chief curator of architecture and design, called it 'our *Winged Victory*', comparing it to the ancient Greek sculpture at the Louvre.

The Museum of Modern Art acquired a Bell-47D-1 helicopter for its collection in 1984, putting the institution in the vanguard of recognizing industrial design aesthetics. Suspending the aircraft over a public staircase, however, took even more nerve.

CHARGING BULL

A symbol of 1980s New York – bold,
confident and unstoppable

As far as New York City tourist attractions go, the *Charging Bull* in Lower Manhattan is a not-so-small capsule of the urban id. Weighing over 2.7t (3 s.t.) and stretching 5.5m (18ft) long, the bronze bovine represents a massive crouching beast with nostrils a-flare and tail twitching. And as an unstoppable brute force is pretty much just how the city likes to see itself.

The creation story of the *Charging Bull* is pure New York as well. It was forged by Arturo Di Modica, a sculptor who emigrated from Italy to SoHo in 1973. Following the stock market crash of 1987, he wanted to make something to celebrate American resilience. He spent two years making the bull. It would be a gift to his adopted city, although at the time it looked a bit more like vandalism. In the dead of a wintry dawn, after staking out the police on their beat and figuring he had four minutes to act, the artist and his friends dropped off the sculpture in front of the New York Stock Exchange on Wall Street where there happened to be a Christmas tree.

A blizzard of media celebrated its abrupt arrival. Under the circumstances, then-Mayor Edward Koch and parks commissioner Harold Stern decided it would be wise to accept this uninvited, un-permitted addition to the public streetscape. However, within two days they had it hauled off to a traffic island a few blocks away on Broadway and Morris Streets. The artist forged more bulls, and, tellingly, a new bull that Di Modica described as 'younger' and 'stronger' was installed in Shanghai in 2010.

Originally a prank and unsolicited gift from a recent Italian émigré sculptor, the bronze bull of Wall Street – actually Morris and Broadway – is now an indelible piece of the downtown landscape and one of its most popular photo opportunities.

NATIONAL DEBT CLOCK
Counting the cost of America's debt

Numerologists and other believers in the power of digits may attribute it to pure voodoo economics (aka Reaganomics) that the National Debt Clock, ratcheting away in Midtown, was first installed in 1989.

It was the brainteaser conceit of real-estate developer Seymour Durst who personally researched and uploaded the numbers to a dot-based segment display (replaced in 2004 by faster LEDs) until his death in 1995.

Now racing past $18 trillion, the National Debt Clock stood at $2.7 trillion when Durst first determined to alert taxpayers to the total debt along with numbers indicating their own slice of responsibility. It cost him $100,000 to install the 3-m x 7.6-m (10-ft x 25-ft) billboard, which was originally located a block from Times Square and then later moved to its present location at 1133 Avenue of the Americas.

In 2000 the clock stopped; the national debt was actually decreasing and the clock was not equipped to run backwards. It started up again in 2002 at $6.1 trillion and caused a brief, unfounded news flurry when it reached $10 trillion in 2008 and the clock seemed to have run out of digits.

The National Debt Clock is not the only counter around. In Union Square there is the Metronome, a 1999 art installation by Kristin Jones and Andrew Ginzel with a 15-space digital clock investigating the 'nature of time' by simultaneously ticking off the seconds, minutes and hours until and away from midnight.

It's 10 p.m. – do you know where your national debt stands? Since 1989, thanks to the National Debt Clock now at 1133 Avenue of the Americas at 44th Street, New Yorkers know at a glance.

CHELSEA MARKET
The chequered past of a gourmet food market

The success of Chelsea Market is one of the more quirky tales of dereliction to destination, and one that is all too rare in a city that would rather reinvent itself from new whole cloth.

In the heart of Chelsea at 15th Street and Ninth Avenue, the block-long red-brick industrial Romanesque factory was built in the 1890s out of a patchwork of bakeries that coalesced into the National Biscuit Company, later Nabisco, manufacturers of such irreducible treats as Saltines, Uneeda biscuits and Oreos, broken crumbs of which were handed out free to neighbourhood kids during the Depression.

After the corporate cookie maker left for New Jersey in the 1950s, the building was taken over by small machine shops and other low-rent habitués associated with Chelsea at the time. In the 1990s a local developer, Ira Cohen, transformed the place into a food hall, preserving its brick arches, cedar columns and factory clerestories and adding such oddities as a 7.3-m (24-ft) granite well with piped-in water from an underground stream and decorative cast-iron body parts donated in lieu of rent by an artist, Mark Mennin, working on the premises.

Now the market is chock-a-block with artisanal and gourmet food purveyors lining a 244-m (800-ft) concourse, the longest interior promenade in the city. Media companies and film studios fill the floors above. Some 6 million visitors funnel through each year. Chelsea Market is one of only two structures that the landscaped elevated park, the High Line, passes right through. It is nice to think that the popular park, the market and the entire neighbourhood of Chelsea achieved their current widespread appeal in large part thanks to their original extreme idiosyncrasies.

What was once the Nabisco cookie factory serving broken crumbs to neighbourhood kids during the Depression is now a mecca for foodies and tourists hosting over 30 wholesale and artisanal craft vendors.

TIFFANY BLUE
A blue so distinct it has its own trademark

It was a stroke of branding genius before branding existed. In 1837 Charles Lewis Tiffany and his original business partner, John Young, opened a stationery and fancy-goods store on Broadway across from City Hall Park. From the start, publicity stunts and clever merchandising went hand in hand, from presenting a miniature silver-filigree horse and carriage as a wedding present to circus performer Tom Thumb and his bride to packing all goods made by Tiffany & Co. (even the solid-gold chamber pot that Diamond Jim Brady ordered up for actress Lillian Russell) in a blue box with a white silk ribbon. Tiffany probably chose a robust robin's-egg blue to conjure turquoise gemstones, popular at the time for friendship pins given to bridesmaids at weddings.

Tiffany & Co. and the Gilded Age rose together, with the store dedicating itself to cultivating the new rich and curating their desires for quality goods in terms of jewellery, china, crystal, silverware, watches and Chinese trinkets. In 1845 Tiffany himself oversaw the creation of the distinctively coloured *Blue Book*, the country's first retail catalogue.

Branch stores opened in London and Paris. Stanford White designed a Venetian palazzo on 37th Street and Fifth Avenue in 1905. (The store ultimately settled for good at 57th and Fifth.) By then, Tiffany & Co. had used blue to seal its association with the luxury of the special occasion, however big or small. Tiffany & Co. then trademarked both the blue colour and the blue box. It appears on no commercial colour wheels, and even Pantone, the industry standard for matching colours, designates it with a dedicated number outside its system – Pantone 1837 – in reference to the year Tiffany opened.

The white satin ribbon and the elegant font speak to expensive taste but nothing quite says luxury in precisely the same way as that distinctive Tiffany's blue box.

TIFFANY & CO.

NEW YORK SINCE 1837

TKTS BOOTH

Father Duffy Square's own stairway to the stars

It could be the plot of a Broadway musical: two young unknowns from Down Under win an international competition to show their stuff on that world-renowned public stage, Times Square.

And it is true. In 1999 two young Australian architects, John Choi and Tai Ropiha, won the design competition to reimagine TKTS, the popular discount ticket sales booth, with their concept for a wedge of glowing red stairs rising 4.8m (16ft) above Father Duffy Square at the northern end of the famous crossroads of Broadway and Seventh Avenue.

But the story of TKTS goes back even further, to 1973 when the city was bankrupt and Broadway was going desperately dark. The Theater Development Group set up a rented construction trailer dressed up with scaffolding wrapped in the TKTS logo to sell extreme discount tickets on the day of performances. By 2000 over 50 million tickets had been sold and the snaking lines of footsore people, kept in line by little more than determination and the Naked Cowboy strumming on a guitar, had become a fixture in Times Square.

It took nine years and $16 million dollars for the new TKTS booth to be completed as realized by New York City architects Perkins Eastman, who made the stair structure and risers entirely of glass illuminated by ruby-red LEDs with a fibreglass shell for 12 ticket kiosks tucked beneath (and warmed by radiant heating that helps melt ice and snow on the stairs).

Today there are additional TKTS venues in Lower Manhattan and Brooklyn where the lines are much shorter, but the TKTS booth in Father Duffy Square still offers the best free seats for watching the neon-jazzed life of the city.

The TKTS booth – selling discount tickets on a first come, first serve basis – takes the more than metaphorical shape of a crimson glass staircase rising at the red hot centre of the Theater District in Times Square.

NATIONAL SEPTEMBER 11 MEMORIAL & MUSEUM

Memorial on a grand scale

Symbols and metaphors are plentiful at the National September 11 Memorial & Museum in downtown Manhattan. And as the plans are realized for four office towers, over half-a-million square feet of retail space and a major transit terminal gradually reabsorbing the site back into the city, they take on even greater significance in commemorating the tragic events of that day.

There are the two deep wells, whose parapets are etched with the names of those who died in the attacks, that cascade with water falling into the footprints of the twin towers that stood (approximately) there until 11 September 2001. There is the pinnacle height of 541m (1,776ft), thanks to a boost from a 124-m (408-ft) antenna mast – the imperial measurement representing the date of the United States Declaration of Independence (1776) – at One World Trade Center, initially known as the Freedom Tower. Transplanted to a central spot between the two footprints is the Survivor Tree, a gnarled pear tree charred by the blast but that in the years since has sprouted smooth new limbs. According to the original master plan, there was to be a plaza called 'The Wedge of Light' that would be lit by a sun without shadows on the morning of every September 11 concurrent with the hour the planes struck.

But for many it is the massive slurry wall, then as now, holding back the Hudson River from flooding the foundations of the Twin Towers – visible to visitors as they descend 21m (70ft) along the ramp to the exhibition spaces of the memorial museum beneath the plaza – that is the most convincing and authentic testament to resilience and strength.

The footprint of the World Trade Center's twin towers inspired the two waterfalls of the National September 11 Memorial & Museum that are each almost an acre (0.4ha) in size and fall 18m (60ft), in two stages.

NEW YORK TIMES LOGO
Echoes of the city's German heritage

The heavy-duty typeface that is the *New York Times* newspaper logo – more properly, its nameplate – is well suited to the central place held by the newspaper in the collective psyche of the city. It manages to look dominant and traditional but also elaborately detailed all at once. Originally named the *New-York Daily Times*, the newspaper and nameplate both settled into the name and look we recognize today in 1857, while losing the hyphen in 1896. The vaguely Germanic shape of the so-called blackletter font, a 17th-century style composed with thick and thin lines, was a plausible choice in the mid-19th century at a time when the city's population was 25 per cent German. In 1869 the *New-York Daily Times* was even printing a German language supplement to each edition.

With each letter drawn freehand, the *New York Times* nameplate belongs to no existing historical font; the closest match is called English Towne. In fact, only the letters of the newspaper name, plus additionally commissioned letters for new words used in titles – including 'magazine' for instance – exist. A marvel of graphic consistency, the logo has generated such devoted brand loyalty that a minor tweaking in 1967 by famed typographer Ed Benguiat triggered wide subscriber rage and is said to have resulted in thousands of cancelled subscriptions. The offence? Removal of a full point and the slimming of the profile.

The newspaper's motto, 'All the news that's fit to print', was adopted in 1896, but the Germanic blackletter font for the *New York Times* nameplate was fixed even earlier in 1857, and has always been drawn freehand.

ANTHORA COFFEE CUP

A morning-meeting staple, now a symbol
of the city that never sleeps

Whether crumpled in a trashcan or stacked on the shelves of the
Museum of Modern Art design store, the New York coffee cup is
instantly recognizable with its white-on-blue stencil, Greek key trim
and three golden cups of steaming brew beneath the chiselled
message, 'We are happy to serve you.'

It is the paper to-go cup that launched a thousand Manhattan
meetings (every morning) and served as instant shorthand for
readymade New York attitude on innumerable television shows
from *NYPD Blue* to *Mad Men*.

Leslie Buck designed the paper coffee cup in 1963 as a
gimmick to appeal to the Greeks who had taken ownership of
many of the city's coffee shops. Buck (originally Laszlo Büch,
a concentration camp survivor from Ukraine) was an executive
of the Sherri Cup Company in Connecticut. He made the cup blue
and white like the Greek flag, added amphora-shaped vessels to
the seams and called it the Anthora. It was an instant success.

At its peak in 2004, the company sold 500 million of the cups
before merging into the Solo Cup Company. Ultimately, the cup
design was retired from active sales, and took up a profitable new
life as an iconic graphic appearing on key chains, cufflinks and
ceramic mugs. Sightings of the real thing have become rare these
days, as are the Greek diners themselves.

Let Starbucks flaunt its bed-
head siren, the most famous
coffee-to-go cup is still the
blue, white and steamy gold
Greek diner paper coffee cup
designed in 1963.

VILLAGE CIGAR STORE
Proof of the value of New York soil

If the scene is set in Greenwich Village, New York, the pressed metal italics on a painted red field proclaiming the Village Cigar Store are bound to be in the establishing shot. The tiny triangular smokes shop has anchored the intersection of Seventh Avenue and Christopher Street since 1938 and maintains its reputation for selling quality cigars from Central and South America with just the right whiff of seedy flair.

But that is only part of the story. Embedded in the sidewalk at the entrance is a black-and-yellow mosaic bearing the adamant inscription 'Property of the Hess Estate which has never been dedicated for public purposes'. This triangular patch, roughly the size of a manhole cover, is the smallest privately owned lot in New York City to have been fought over in court. (There are actually seven other privately owned slices that are even smaller.)

It happened back in the early 20th century, when the city moved to extend Seventh Avenue, and beneath it the IRT subway line. In the Village that meant taking possession of and demolishing 300 buildings. The Hess family of Philadelphia went to court to try and save a five-storey apartment building they owned on the corner at Christopher Street, but lost all but a tiny remnant. The city assumed that that piece would be donated to become part of the public sidewalk. No, said David Hess, who returned to court and won the battle for ownership that he commemorated on 27 July 1922 with the mosaic plaque, cracked but still perfectly legible today.

Filmmakers have long relied on establishing shots of the red, white and crazy signage at Village Cigars to tell moviegoers, 'We are now in Greenwich Village'.

EAGLE WAREHOUSE
The point that Brooklyn's fortunes turned?

Trying to pinpoint when Brooklyn turned from sleepy outer borough to inner sanctum of urban cool is a matter of conjecture. The shutting down of the Domino Sugar Refinery in 2004 is one possible, if late, date. There is 1978 when Brooklynites coined the name DUMBO for Down Under the Manhattan Bridge Overpass to put off prospective developers, although that could be apocryphal.

Then there is the conversion of the Eagle Warehouse & Storage Company, witness and partner to Brooklyn's original heyday in the late 1890s and now a condominium at the white-hot centre of the waterfront's revival, its fortress-style parapet set with a gigantic glass clock face visible to all who cross over the Brooklyn Bridge from Manhattan.

The Eagle Warehouse at 28 Old Fulton Street was named for and built in 1894 on the site of the *Brooklyn Eagle* newspaper, where Walt Whitman was a contributor and editor in the 1840s. In fact, the old pressroom was incorporated into the new structure designed by Frank Freeman, who worked in motifs from the medieval to the Romanesque and was considered Brooklyn's finest architect. The Brooklyn Bridge spelled the demise of the area known as Fulton Landing that had depended on ferry traffic and manufacturing.

That is, until the late 20th century when all the red-brick masonry, stone arches and leaded-glass factory windows exerted their appeal on a new generation of homesteaders. In 1980 the Eagle Warehouse was converted into rental apartments, with one-bedrooms with 9.5-m- (31-ft-) long living rooms renting for $800 a month. Then, as now, a studio apartment with views looking out from behind the glass clock is considered one of the most desirable places to live in New York City.

Once a storage facility now a deluxe condominium, the Eagle Warehouse has always had great bones and medieval detailing. The glass clock in the parapet (below) looks into the home of an architect and interior designer, Michael Davis.

CHINESE REFLEXOLOGY CHARTS
A sign of New York's affordable luxuries

There is the subway map that New Yorkers consult grudgingly when they want to check how close the E train from Queen's Plaza gets to Columbus Circle, and then there is the Chinese reflexology foot chart. Whether the chart is colour-coded like a world globe from seventh-grade geography or a classic anatomy section, it is plain to see that the connection between tender insole and the kidneys or base of the little toe and shoulder is much more direct. What idling town cars are to the city's one-percenters, foot massages are for the hard-charging masses – an affordable luxury with a tincture of the exotic.

In 1971 *New York* magazine noted the new craze for acupuncture, followed by feature coverage in *Time* and *Life* and photographs of actress Julie Christie getting the treatment in *Vogue*. In those days, there were only a few licensed practitioners in the United States. New York led the charge and today there are well over 90 traditional Chinese medical practices in Manhattan, and untold hundreds of Chinese massage parlours, instantly recognizable by the foot and hand charts in the window.

This is hardly surprising as the New York metropolitan area is home to the largest population of ethnic Chinese outside Asia, numbering 735,019 as of 2012. There are nine Chinatowns: the original one in Lower Manhattan plus three in Queens, three in Brooklyn and one each in Nassau County, Long Island and in Edison, New Jersey. For a city full of hardcore walkers – more than a few in stiletto heels – there is always a treatment parlour where for $30 or less they can find immediate temporary relief.

New York is a city of immigrants and walkers. The two merge in Chinatown, where basement boutiques offer deep-tissue massage according to ancient medicinal custom. Just follow the neon feet signs.

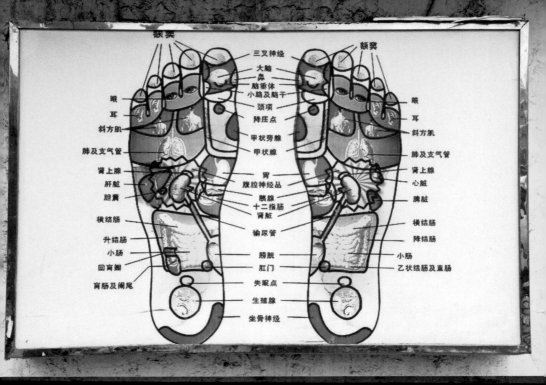

HEARST TOWER
A rare restrained voice among the city's towers

The Hearst Tower by Norman Foster + Partners represents a most unusual achievement in a city known for striving to outdo itself – the restrained skyscraper. At 182m (597ft) and 46 storeys, it does not even rank among the 100 tallest buildings in New York.

It stands out all the more for the distinctive zigzag profile of its monumental diagonal bracing – each zig and zag extends four storeys – and the way that it scissor-lifts up from within an art deco cast-stone base. Building on top of a landmark – the headquarters for press lord William Randolph Hearst designed with theatrical urns-and-garlands detailing by Viennese architect Joseph Urban in 1928 – was only one challenge.

The Hearst Tower was also the first skyscraper approved for construction following the attacks of 11 September 2001. Completed in 2005, it is Norman Foster's first building in the United States and it is loaded with sustainable features that may happily be commonplace now but were record-setting innovations at the time, from using 21 per cent less steel than comparable towers to radiant heated limestone floors using water collected on the roof. A three-storey glass waterfall in the lobby traversed by elevators makes arrival an entirely new experience but also works to thermally condition and cool the building. Maybe the Hearst Tower is a bit stubby but it makes a strong case for showing that a powerful impression does not have to be about height.

Hearst media empire's HQ building in Midtown, completed in 2005, was British architect Norman Foster's first building in the United States. For New York, it was the first thoroughly green skyscraper, if only 46 storeys tall.

NYPL LIONS

'Patience' and 'Fortitude', true New Yorkers through thick and thin

In 2008 the majestic New York Public Library on Fifth Avenue announced that it would undergo a name change, becoming the Stephen A Schwartzman Building in honour of the billionaire's donation of $100 million towards an ambitious renovation, substantially derailed by public protest in 2014.

Meanwhile, the two Tennessee marble lions that flank the grand staircase to the Beaux-Arts stunner have been rebranded a few times themselves. In 1911, when the Carrère and Hastings–designed library opened, the two lions were called 'Leo Astor' and 'Leo Lenox' after founders John Jacob Astor and James Lenox, whose private libraries comprised the new public collection, but were often referred to as 'Lady Astor' and 'Lord Lenox'. The lions were modelled by Edward Clark Potter, a noted sculptor at the time, and carved by the Bronx-based Piccirilli Brothers who also carved the *Abraham Lincoln* sitting within the Lincoln Memorial in Washington, DC.

New Yorkers have long embraced the lions as their own with a tradition of adorning the felines on festive occasions with holly wreaths, mortarboards and top hats. During the 1930s Depression, Mayor Fiorello H La Guardia renamed the lions again in an effort to boost local morale, calling them 'Patience' and 'Fortitude'. And the names have stuck. In fact, the library has trademarked the cats as its official logo and mascots. In 2004, at the advice of conservators, however, the tradition of adorning 'Patience' and 'Fortitude' was discontinued.

After the Library of Congress, the New York Public Library has the largest book collection in the country, and third largest in the world. But it is the two marble lion mascots on the steps that New Yorkers love.

8 SPRUCE STREET
Frank Gehry scales new heights

In 2011 it was billed as the tallest residential tower in the western hemisphere but that didn't last long as supertalls became the new normal throughout New York and the world. But the 76-storey 8 Spruce Street will always be world-famous architect Frank Gehry's first skyscraper. And his second building completed in New York following numerous high-profile false starts and the completion in 2007 of the cool, iceberg-shaped IAC headquarters on the West Side Highway.

In the early years of the 21st century, Frank Gehry's name was attached to many of the city's most aspirational plans, from the competition for a new headquarters for the *New York Times* (Gehry withdrew) to an $850-million new Guggenheim Museum on the East River near the Brooklyn Bridge (dropped in 2002). In the aftermath of the September 11 attacks, Gehry's was the only name considered for a world-class performing arts centre at 'Ground Zero', shelved in 2014.

'New York by Gehry', as the tower's developers pitched it, has been a critical success. Its 900 rental apartments have views stretching from the Brooklyn Bridge to Coney Island. The building is clad in a stainless steel that appears to ripple like the drapery on ancient statues, or like 'Bernini folds' according to the architect. With one of the most distinctive façades in the city, 8 Spruce is considered a worthy neighbour to another standout tower, the neo-gothic Woolworth Building of 1913.

Encased in rippling folds of stainless steel, the 76-storey tower designed by Frank Gehry streaks past the stately spires of the 57-storey Woolworth Building that has long anchored this lower Manhattan neighbourhood around City Hall.

HIGH LINE

A NYC fairy tale, saved from demolition at the
very last minute

From high-voltage threat and industrial eyesore to one of the
most celebrated new parks in the world, the High Line captures
better than any other icon the mercurial nature of success and
popularity in this demanding city. The elevated railroad viaduct
was built in the 1930s to carry freight from the Pennsylvania rail
yards to the warehouses of Greenwich Village. By 1980 that
service was obsolete and the tracks just 9–18m (30–60ft) wide
and some 9m (30ft) above the street were abandoned to all but
the desperate and the adventuresome.

On the eve of demolition by popular demand, a neighbourhood
group of writers and artists in Chelsea rallied to its passionate
defence armed with romantic photographs of the tangle of wild
overgrowth that had overtaken the tracks. An international
competition flushed out ideas from the inspired to the inane (one
proposal suggested turning the entire 2.4-km (1.5-mile) length into
a swimming pool). Ultimately, a team led by landscape firm Field
Operations laid in a highly cultivated landscape invoking rails
gone wild to seed. The thrill of viewing the city from a height while
strolling through sweeping moor grasses and flowering quince,
flyover grated bridges and railroad-tie bleachers proved irresistibly
entrancing. After opening in 2009, some 3 million visitors a year
were thronging the High Line; and real-estate values along its
edges quadrupled. In 2014, at a cost of over $155 million (making
it one of the most expensive parks per square foot ever built),
the final section of the High Line was completed and there was
barely a city in the world that wasn't taking a closer look at its own
derelict rail extensions as a potential urban-renewal gold mine.

Even with its art galleries,
Chelsea, neither up- nor
downtown between Midtown
and the Village, was slow
to catch on until the High
Line, an abandoned railroad
transformed into high-design
park, made it a tourist
destination.

ZUCCOTTI PARK
The home of Occupy Wall Street

Originally named Liberty Plaza Park, Zuccotti Park has since become famous as the granite-paved strip between Broadway and Church at Liberty Street where the protest group known as Occupy Wall Street (OWS) set up their camp in the autumn of 2011.

The choice of Zuccotti Park was no coincidence. Not only is Wall Street two blocks away but Zuccotti Park also turns out to be one of the city's little-understood POPS, or 'privately owned public spaces'. There are over 520 POPS around the city, often adjacent to the corporate towers that created them as concessions to building taller. The Pittsburgh-based US Steel installed Liberty Plaza Park in 1968 as an added obligation mandated by 1961 zoning laws. Unlike public parks that close at curfew or POPS designated in later years that close from dusk to dawn, Liberty Park would be kept open 24 hours a day. In 2006 new owners renamed it Zuccotti Park.

It is said that the OWS organizers had planned to take over Chase Manhattan Plaza, more symbolically potent when targeting banks, but it was closed. Perhaps it was an urban planner among them who alerted them to the technicality that made it very difficult to dislodge protesters from what they insisted on calling, once again, Liberty Park. Meeting tents, a kitchen, a generator and even a library were all part of the OWS encampment for over two months before a court order forced them to leave. A clash on New Year's Eve 2011 between 500 'We kick the ass of the ruling class' protesters and the NYPD was the last confrontation before the movement subsided and Zuccotti Park resumed its life as a lunchtime retreat for office workers.

Thanks to a real-estate loophole keeping it open to the public 24/7, Zuccotti Park – two blocks east of 'Ground Zero' – made a perfect camping ground for the OWS protesters in October 2011.

FOUR FREEDOMS PARK

Roosevelt's NYC monument, one of the
final works of Louis I Kahn

Due east of the United Nations and cleaving the East River's swift currents, the southern prow of Roosevelt Island is encased in 33-t (36-s.t.) blocks of granite chiselled to an exacting 1.8 x 1.8 x 3.6m (6 x 6 x 12ft). Aligned but not touching, the blocks – placed by tipping into sand as the ancient Egyptians did – form a square room open to the skies. The room also opens forward to the river and backwards to a chevron-shaped lawn lined with diverging *alleés* of lime trees ending in a grand staircase. The lawn is buttressed by monumental granite ramps and a riprap soaking up the river. This is the FDR Four Freedoms Park, a monument to Franklin Delano Roosevelt designed by the pre-eminent American architect Louis I Kahn in 1974 but not built until 2012. There is probably no spot more serene or more removed from the barrelling life of the city.

Roosevelt Island sits on a narrow stretch of the river between Manhattan and Queens. Formerly known as Welfare Island and used as a quarry, a prison and an asylum, the island was rededicated to Roosevelt in 1973 by Mayor John Lindsay as he announced the future memorial. The financial collapse of the city in 1975 and then changing political will derailed the project for several decades.

The only memorial in town to Roosevelt and one of Kahn's very last works, the Four Freedoms Park is now deemed one of the city's most significant works of architecture.

Louis I Kahn, one of the most universally revered of modernist architects, designed a monument to Franklin Delano Roosevelt that took over 38 years to be built, long after both men had died, on an island in sight of the United Nations.

BARCLAYS CENTER
A controversial exercise in scale

The Barclays Center is a swooping behemoth of customized technology and artfully woven form – every one of its 12,000 rusted panels is different. When the sports arena was completed in 2012, Barclays clinched the transformation of upwardly mobile Prospect Heights from tight-knit Brooklyn community to celebrated urban magnet. Barclays is home to the Nets basketball team (bought by Russian oligarch Mikhail Prokhorov in 2010) and an entertainment venue with seating for up to 19,000. It sits at the prow of a 9-ha (22-acre) development atop an old rail yard that will eventually include 16 residential, office and hotel towers.

The neighbourhood fought famously long and hard to block the controversial project that originally involved the forced removal of residents as well as a more expansive design by Frank Gehry. By 2009, however, Gehry's oversight was reduced to just the master plan, and SHoP Architects together with AECOM stepped in with a less expensive, more workable, but still clever design. It includes a 32-storey prefabricated tower slated to be the world's tallest modular building, constructed at the nearby Brooklyn Navy Yard. While the pre-fab tower has struggled to completion, belying the notion that modular can be fast and feasible at any scale, the Barclays arena has been a tremendous hit. In 2013 it ranked second in the world for tickets sold, following the O2 in London.

Building a sports arena in an urban neighbourhood is one of those projects that developers consider a dream of economic profitability but locals deem a nightmare of congestion. Barclays promised Brooklynites both.

INDEX

PICTURE CREDITS

CREDITS

An Hachette UK Company
www.hachette.co.uk

First published in
Great Britain in 2015
by Conran Octopus,
a division of Octopus
Publishing Group Ltd,
in conjunction with the
Design Museum

Octopus Publishing Group
Ltd
Carmelite House
50 Victoria Embankment
London EC4Y 0DZ
www.octopusbooks.co.uk
www.octopusbooksusa.com

Distributed in the US by
Hachette Book Group
1290 Avenue of the
Americas, 4th and 5th Floors,
New York, NY 10020

Distributed in Canada by
Canadian Manda Group
664 Annette St., Toronto,
Ontario, Canada M6S 2C8

A CIP catalogue record
for this book is available
from the British Library.

Text written by:
Julie Iovine

Commissioning Editor:
Joe Cottington
Consultant Editor:
Deyan Sudjic
Senior Editor:
Alex Stetter
Copy Editor:
Robert Anderson
Design:
Untitled
Picture Researcher:
Claire Gouldstone
Production Controller:
Allison Gonsalves

Based on a concept by
Hugh Devlin

Printed and bound in China
ISBN 978 1 84091 691 1

10 9 8 7 6 5 4 3 2 1